Living Growing Healing

Eleanor Gray

BookLeaf
Publishing

India | USA | UK

Presentation by *BookLeaf Publishing*

Web: www.bookleafpub.com

E-mail: info@bookleafpub.com

ISBN: 9789358312553

First edition 2023

ACKNOWLEDGEMENT

Most importantly, I want to thank my mother, Jodie, and my fiancé, Ty. These two people have been unwavering beacons of support and patience as I have tried to navigate this confusing and overwhelming thing called Life. I also want to thank my closest friends, Zoe, Sara, and Max, for showing me what true friendship is and always pushing me to be my best self. Without this support, I truly don't think I'd be where I am today, or able to share this in the way I am. These people have taught me the beauty of being my authentic self and the joy that comes with being loved for who you really are. Without these influences in my life I wouldn't feel safe or worthy to share my work. Next, I want to thank every single person who has come and gone from my life, because my experiences with you have shaped who I am today. Even the bad ones I am grateful for, because they taught me valuable lessons and made me stronger today. If you read this, I hope you read it with an open mind. Finally, I want to thank Book Leaf Publishinf Co., for allowing me this opportunity to speak my truth.

PREFACE

Some of these poems will be very personal, and there will be topics such as domestic and sexual abuse, gender and sexual identity, mental illness, and just raw emotion. Read at your own risk.

The Poets

Contrary to popular belief,
Poets do not usually live poetic lives
The world continues to burn and it's
Story is told by whoever survives

What an arduous task for someone
Burdened with the gift of verse
To write about the beauty of life
When the reality is often so much worse

Perhaps that is the beauty by itself
To know that there is no life without pain
Yet still put the pen to paper in attempts
To leave on this world a noticeable stain

For one day when everything you know
Has returned from whence it came
We will all be one with ash and dust and
Only the words we wrote will remain the same

When hundreds of years from now
They wonder what our lives were like
It won't be the surgeons or lawmen they'll look
for
But the words of authors and poets they'll find

Without writers we have no history to learn from
Without poets, nothing to confront how we feel
Without the knowledge of those who came
before us
There is so much less hope, so little ideal

We must not be afraid to speak our minds
To stand up for what we think is right
If we do not cooperate against the darkness
We will lose the battle to preserve the light

We cannot lose sight of what we have learned
Or let the world dampen our creativity
We will keep writing for what we believe in
Giving the power of rhyme to our sensitivity

Sometimes the world's cruelty consumes
The hope and love we hold dear
And we are left with nothing but
A pit of ravenous fear

Doesn't it all seem so pointless then?
To keep pushing through the struggle of life
To keep searching for reasons to be good
When the reasons not to be cut like a knife

But they are there, I promise you
Just look at the stars as they rise

Feel the embrace of someone you love
Let the years teach you how to be wise

Because there is beauty in the way we live
There is comfort in the ebb and flow
Even when you feel you will always be down
Just wait it out and up you will go

Let us write about the beautiful and the ugly
Because that is what we were meant to do
We will write about what it is to be human
For those who will wonder what we went
through

You will never take our words away
No matter how hard you try
We will persist in spreading the truth
Up until the day we die

Warm Summer Day

On a warm summer day
All on my own
I'm only nine years old
Already exploring the unknown

"You've always been so independent"
The world's biggest understatement

I grew up my father's daughter
I wore my heart on my sleeve
And then he was the first man
To make my arms bleed

Do you see all the fear I hold?
Do you know of the peace he stole?

I never was good at making friends
Even worse at making them stay
I felt an ugliness within myself
I only seemed to push them away

And I was just a child
Yet somehow still reviled

Do you ever wonder what it would be like

If just one little thing had gone differently?
Like what if your dad never drank
And gave you love consistently

Would my mind be quiet then?
Could I do it all over again?

All I ever wanted was to be
Unconditionally loved
All I ever seemed to get was
Unfairly judged

Always held to such high expectations
And never given much consideration

I never liked being told what to do,
I always thought I was smarter
I had made it so far on my own,
I knew I'd be fine going farther

Even though I've always been misunderstood
I've gotten farther than anyone thought I could

My childhood is long since over
Even if sometimes I still cling to the past
The child I was still lives within me
Deep within me her pain amassed

I am here now, I feel you hurting

Please take my comfort, you are deserving

I will never let you go hungry
And I will always brush your hair
I cross my heart and hope to die
I'll be here for you, forever, I swear

I will heal my child self's injuries
I will let go of my past self's miseries

On a warm summer day
All on my own
I'm nineteen years old
And I'm no longer alone

Dear Father

Dear Father,
There was once a time I saw you as a hero
Fighting for our freedom, or at least it appeared
so
You should have kept the violence on the front
lines
But you were the violence, invading the confines
Of our home, always a lurking sense of danger
The loving man I thought I knew became a
stranger
Splintered wood, glass broken on the floor
An army soldier who brought home the war
My mother didn't think that I could tell
That her bruises weren't just because "she fell"
Sitting on the top step while you're downstairs
screaming
Now I'm wondering if the word "love" has any
meaning
My father, the soldier, you were supposed to
protect us
Now you're the reason that I hold so much
distrust
Choosing to stay was my biggest mistake
You weren't supposed to my first heartbreak
You're not the man I thought you'd be

Why couldn't you keep your hands off of me
You were supposed to keep me safe from bad
men's hands
You had no right to touch me in ways I didn't
understand
It's been years and you're still running from the
truth
Trying to deny what you did to me in my youth
You can say it was all made up by my mother
But I vividly remember the ways you made me
suffer
There will come a time when it will all catch up
to you
And everyone will know what you put me
through
So be afraid, you're not invincible
And nothing you've done is fixable
You're not my father, you've been abandoned
Just like you did to me, Brandon

The Right People

If there's one thing you should know about me
It's that I can be quite intense
I feel a lot and that has caused
A lot of issues with my friends

When I was younger it always seemed
Like everyone was out to get me
I seemed to have a reputation
Even with people who never met me

They called me dramatic, irrational,
Sometimes even crazy
It took me a while to not see myself
How so many others see me

I tried to recognize the patterns
And fix the problem before it began
But eventually I realized that
The problem was the way I am

My opinions were too strong
I couldn't hide the way I felt
I struggled to cope with
The cards that I was dealt

Maybe I was sometimes too loud
Maybe they saw me as a threat
I didn't mean to care so much
I didn't want to make anyone upset

All I wanted was a companion
Someone to trust and to confide in
Someone that would always have my back
A friendship that I could take pride in

I wanted to give up completely
And give into the distrust
Maybe I didn't deserve friendship
Maybe I really was too much

But friendship really is such a gift
A truly beautiful thing
Like smelling breakfast in the morning
Or hearing the birds sing

To know you have someone in your corner
When the whole world can feel against you
To have someone that knows who you really are
Someone that you don't have to pretend to

When you finally meet the right people
You realize that all the wrong ones were worth it
All the pain taught you important lessons
Even when you felt like you didn't deserve it

When you give up being someone you're not
And start prioritizing your own needs
The right people seem to just gravitate towards
you
People you can genuine believe won't leave

The people who care about how you feel
And are interested in how you think
The people you never get tired of being around
Their place in your life feels like instinct

There are few people who stick around forever
And it can be hard to accept that
But sometimes it is better to live
Just with someone's lasting impact

Dear Mother

Dear Mother,
Nobody knows your heart like I do
Because it beats inside of me
And no matter what we go through
Your love is all I see
You once told me your pain
Was nothing compared to mine
But I think that's insane
I think your pride has made you blind
You say I am strong
But I think you are stronger
My sufferings have lasted long
But yours have lasted longer
And I know it's yourself you blame
For the things he did to me
I know what my childhood became
Was not what you wanted it to be
But I think the best thing you did was leave
You had to do it for yourself
You showed me, and I still believe
That self-respect is the greatest wealth
You've always pushed me to do my best
You say you don't want me to turn out like you
But I think that's a lie just like the rest
You were the first woman I ever looked up to

And I need you to understand that
You aren't defined by the mistakes you made
It only matters where your heart is at
By love your failures are outweighed
You are my mother but you are human first
That's not something I always understood
And even though I showed you my worst
You always did the best you could
I will never be able to thank you enough
For every sacrifice
I know raising me was tough
And I apologize
I know how proud of me you are
But please never forget
You're the reason I've gotten this far
And I can never repay that debt
Instead what I am going to do
Is immortalize it all in writing
So you won't forget that I love you
Even when we're fighting

Girl On Fire

I've spent a lot of my years full of rage
Boiling hot tar bubbling in my insides, always
threatening to spill over
Did I learn this from my dad or was I born this
way?
There is a fire burning in me, breathing with me,
an eternal solar
But they say there's always something
underneath
A hard exterior to shield you from your fears
Years of hurt and disappointment building up
Because sometimes screaming feels better than
tears
And there are many my fire has burned
Some did and some didn't deserve it
But eventually I had to learn
That lashing out was never worth it
The fire that burns within me, it cannot be
extinguished
The unrelenting force inside me cannot be
relinquished
But I cannot live like this forever, I refuse to be
fueled by hate
Obsession does nothing other than put me in a
dismal state

There must be something I can do
Some way to circumvent
The energy this fire provides
So it can be better spent
I will always be full of passion
Instilled with a deep concern for the unjust
But I can no longer let it cloud my judgement
I can no longer allow it to fuel my distrust
There are things that I will never understand,
some people from which I will never receive
closure
And there are mistakes I made that I will never
be able to do over
But not learning from the past will only make it
repeat itself
An unavoidable consequence of our stupidity
I cannot just forget all of my pain and move on
But neither can I continue to wallow in self-pity
Now is the time I invest in myself
My success, my comfort, my healing
I'll surround myself with people who respect me
And care about how I'm feeling
I will be patient and forgiving with myself
As well as with the world around me
I will no longer let myself be controlled
By my fear and insecurity
I used to feel like I had something to prove
To all of those that hate me

But I no longer care what they think of my
progress
It's those I love that motivate me
This fire is nothing I need to be ashamed of
As long as I can keep it under control
There is a comfort to its warmth, it gives me
radiance
It gives me the strength I need to bare my soul
I must learn to harness this inferno
From the shackles of my anger I must be free
For I do not serve my anger
Rather, my anger serves me

Divine Feminine

I am a woman in the way my body is a temple
that deserves to be worshipped
I align with femininity in the way I keep my hair
long and my nails clipped
My girlhood cannot be separated from my
existence
Kept in the core of my belly, an involuntary
subsistence
It is the pleasantness that keeps my soul soft
And the dreaminess that keeps my mind aloft
I am the little girl inside me doting on baby dolls
The little girl that saw the holes the wrath of
men left in the walls
I am a woman in the way my rage is taught by
men
But it runs much deeper than could ever be felt
by them
So go on, enjoy the sweet taste of my femininity
But remember that you are feasting on divinity
You can deny it, but we make the world go
round
We rule silently, we don't need to be crowned
We don't need to be the best just to prove that
we have worth

All these years we've been reduced to cleaning
and giving birth
Yet there is a magic we hold, a soft and gentle
glow
We are beauty manifested no matter where we
go
They have call us emotional, dramatic, intense
But when men do the same things it makes
perfect sense
We have been taught to make ourselves
palatable to others all our lives
Society tells us from the beginning that all we're
meant to be are wives
Men have made it clear all that matters is whats
between our hips
Even when we give them children we still have
to fear the "Husband Stitch"
We must be pleasing to them but we can never
be better
We are only objects meant to benefit the
collector
But we are tired of being carved to fit their
expectations
We are fed up with being left out of all the
conversations
Because we may be emotional, but men are far
too cold
We are beacons of love, we don't care about
control

Our cities were built by the violence of men
By jealousy and fear of the highest extent
So you can continue to say women are too
emotional
But we are taught to deal with our emotions,
While men's are uncontrollable

To Learn To Love

It's hard to learn to love when the first man that
broke your heart was your father
An angry man that taught you that all of your
needs were a bother
The way he talks to your mother makes you start
to think that love might be hopeless
You don't want to fall in love with someone just
as soulless
You think you'll never end up like that but then
your first love blooms
And you wonder why no one told you how much
of you your love consumes
Until you're sacrificing your comfort solely for
the sake of his satisfaction
And when it finally gets too much, you're
demonized for your reaction
When you're young and naive, this love
becomes your routine
You think it's completely normal for his love to
go unseen
You'll start fights in a desperate attempt to feel
important to him
But eventually all your love is is lifeless and
grim

So when something exciting comes along, you
jump at your chance
To feel wanted and important, to experience
romance
He'll be loving and attentive as long as you give
him sex
But all the while he'll be behind your back with
his ex
And when your needs become too much he
becomes aggressive and mean
What a sad thing to feel you have no value at the
ripe age of sixteen
He further instills it in you that your body is all
you're good for
And inside your head the word "love" is now
synonymous with "war"
Then he breaks your heart in two and leaves you
with the rubble
And you come to the conclusion that love is too
much trouble
All you ever really wanted was to feel cared
about
For a love that you could own and not need to
doubt
Not a love that was over before it even begun
Or that made you wonder if you were the only
one
But they always say that true love finds you
when you least expect it

And when it does you should probably do all
you can to protect it
So even though you're full of anger and your
love has been reduced to ashes
You decide to give it one more try with the
sweet boy wearing the nerdy glasses
And even when you hurt him because you think
love needs to be painful
He treats you with understanding instead of
making you feel shameful
He shows you a side of love you didn't think
existed
One where patience and forgiveness is never
restricted
He shows you that real love shouldn't put you
on the offense
And that to be loved should never come at such
great expense
He gives you the strength to be better, gives you
something you can work for
The proof that he loves you isn't something you
have to search for
You are able to learn from your mistakes
because of the safety he provides
You are able to move forward with his love and
commitment as your guides
Because you see how good he tries to be for you
His love makes you feel clean and new

And his effort is something that deserves to be
returned
For him your unhealthy patterns need to be
unlearned
And throughout it all he is on your side
Your expectations of love defied
It took nineteen years to learn to love correctly
But you finally know and feel love that is
healthy

We are Here We are Real We are Valid

I cannot make up how I feel and I did not choose
to be this way
If I could I would have chosen to make this
feeling go away
You think I want to feel uncomfortable in my
own skin?
Why would anyone choose to hate the body
they're in?
We aren't the way we are because we enjoy the
abuse
All we want is for you to be mindful of the
words you use
You can hate us all you want but that doesn't
mean what we are isn't real
You don't have to agree but you're going to have
to learn how to deal
With the fact that we aren't going anywhere no
matter how hard you try
Our peace isn't something we will happily allow
you to deny
My wanting to be comfortable in my body is not
a threat to you
You don't even remotely care that all the things
they say aren't true

We aren't predators and we are not forcing
surgery on kids
You call us sinners but we don't comment on
your many sins
God loves all of His children the same
Even if they take hormones and change their
name
And if he doesn't, why should I dedicate my life
to Him?
How good is a god who condemns people for the
way He created them
And you're mad because you don't want to use
our preferred pronouns?
It's astounding that your ignorance truly knows
no bounds
You justify your hypocrisy by cherry-picking
bible verses
And use them to preach hatred inside your
oh-so-holy churches
If you were truly Christian you would know that
Christ accepts us
You would actually care about how your words
affect us
And when you tell us we're going to Hell out of
hate
Just know that you will suffer the exact same
fate
It is not hard to be kind even when you don't
understand

We deserve to love who we are even if that
means we're damned
It is not your place to tell us what our lives are
worth
Maybe you wouldn't hate us if you did some
real research
If you don't like trans people you don't have to
be friends with any
Compared to the rest of the world there aren't
actually that many
But regardless of how you feel we deserve to
live in peace
We don't deserve to feel unsafe simply walking
down the street
Instead they pass laws dictating our right to life
Do you know how many trans kids have already
died?
It's said that 40% of trans youth attempt to take
their own life
Or they're found in a park brutally murdered
with a knife
There is no excuse for this hate-borne violence
And we will no longer continue to suffer in
silence
I don't want to live the rest of my life in fear
Of it being cut short just because I'm queer
I want to live in a world that values love and
acceptance

And the only thing stopping that is your hateful
misconceptions

Borderline

For you everything is black and white
You've always struggled to find the gray
Everything must be either wrong or right
There cannot be night among the day

You seem to always be teetering on an edge
Trying your best to walk along the line
Every problem feels like life or death
You either see everything or are completely
blind

You don't remember what made you like that
Just that you had to do it to stay alive
Sorting everything into "good" or "bad"
Was the only way you knew how to survive

Because everything seems out to get you
And it always feels so big and scary
And when danger is all you ever knew
You can't afford not to be wary

Now that you've grown up it's become an issue
No one likes the hot and cold
No one can handle being with you
They wish you could keep your anger controlled

But you never knew a safe embrace
You were never able to calm down
You took life at such a fast pace
Always afraid you were going to drown

You tried to grow up fast, you wanted
independence
You thought that would put your pain to an end
Now when you look back on your adolescence
You want to go and do it all over again

You're trying now to be okay with the lukewarm
And to recognize the gray
You're learning to appreciate the calm between
the storms
You're seeing the life that blooms from decay

And even though it's not always easy
There is comfort in knowing things can be both
Eventually you are able to live freely
And find solace in your own growthyou

Two Damaged Souls

We did not love with kindness.
We embraced each other with broken glass
bodies, desperate for a warmth that neither of us
could provide.
We cut into each other instead, leaving wounds
that would scar with resentment we felt was
justified.
Because I was nursed with a wrath that boiled
until it steamed; I was reared with a wickedness
that withered my heart and poisoned my
screams.
And you were fostered with quiet disapproval
that weighed on your heart; you were burdened
with an absence that slowly tore your world
apart.
We were two hurting lovers—naive and
flawed—
Our sweet love untasted, cold and unthawed.
Yet, somehow,
We saved our love from certain death,
Still finding comfort in each other's breath.
We learned how to soften our edges and love
without expectations,
To talk about our feelings and speak out on our
frustrations.

We learned the language our hearts spoke, as
well as the words from inside that it woke.
We taught ourselves how to be patient and
gentle,
How to be honest and warm and sentimental.
You showed me the love I didn't think existed,
You pulled me in from the stormy sea, your hold
on me unresisted.
The sun shines on us as we leave our shells
behind,
Our souls transcending, no longer confined.
For I will love you long past the end of our time,
There is not a sacrifice I wouldn't make, not a
mountain I wouldn't climb,
I would travel across the entire world
Just to have you by my side forevermore.

A Letter To Myself

Hello? Can you hear me?
I know you're trying to push me away
I know how broken you feel right now
Please just listen to what I have to say

You are drowning in your mind
You cannot move on from your mistakes
I can see the guilt and fear you hold
And I know how much it aches

I know the way you strive for perfection
And feel like a failure when you aren't
But I see how hard you try, I promise
I know the good you hold in your heart

Because you are so much more
Than when you're at you're lowest
You can do such beautiful things
When you keep your mind focused

And you are so much better
Than the mistakes you carry
They'll only drag you down
And I know you're feeling weary

You are here for a reason
And you've made it so far
You've put in too much work
To forget all that you are

Aren't you proud of yourself?
You made it all these years
You've learned so many lessons
You kept going despite your fears

I know when it all feels so heavy
It can be easy to forget
All of the darkness is overwhelming
You're swallowed up by the hurt and stress

The doubts in your head
Tell you that you'll amount to nothing
That all of your effort is in vain
And that of love you are undeserving

But you have been through so much
And you are still standing here today
You surpassed everyone's expectations
No matter what anyone had to say

You were given a gift that so many lose
And no matter how cruel life may seem
There are so many reasons to keep going
You still have so much time to dream

There are still so many jokes to laugh at
So many sunsets for you to watch
There's so much music you haven't listened to
There will still be sunny showers in March

You are still able to drink hot tea before bed
And unwind with nice warm bubble baths
You can still dance to music with your friends
And go running barefoot in soft green grass

These small joys can be easy to overlook
When you compare them to your pains
But all the little things add up
And in the end, they're all that remains

One day, when you're old and frail
Looking back on how you spent your life
You'll wonder why you spent so much time
Dwelling on the anger and the strife

When there are so many good things in front of
you
So many things to be grateful for
And you're focusing on what you've lost
Instead of what's in store

You should be proud of how far you've gotten
And for everything you've gotten through

And thankful for the opportunities you've been
given
And for the people who have always been there
for you

So the next time you're relaxing in nature
Feeling the warmth of the sun on your face
Or in bed on a lazy Sunday morning
Safe in the comfort of your lover's embrace

Thank yourself for getting you there
For getting through all that you did
You can be who you want to be
You're no longer just a kid

You deserve to be here
And it's okay to be sad
But you must remember the good
In the midst of all the bad

You must allow yourself to smile
And the enjoy the small joys life brings
Don't let the dark thoughts pull you down
Just rise above and spread your wings

Haunt You

Did you really truly love me?
Or did you just like the taste of my skin
Or rather the sight of my blood as it dripped
Down my thigh after you sunk your teeth in
Did you really truly want me?
Or was the fire you lit in my insides
Only warm enough for you to stand besides
When the cold of the night crept in
Did you really truly see me?
Or was it just what you saw that kept you around
What you could touch and what you could own
I should've known the physical was what kept
you bound
Did you really truly need me?
Or was i only your emergency fix
Maybe you wanted to see how many
Times i'd fall for your overused tricks
You never loved me, or wanted me,
Or saw me, or needed me, and yet here i am
Feeding you more than you can swallow
This is what you asked for and now here i am
Seeing how much you can swallow
Because that's the thing about me is
You'll never quite get rid of the taste
And once i get out of your grasp

You'll regret letting me go to waste
A storm rages inside me
One that you knew well
Your "love" could never calm me
Now i'm your personal hell
Your mother told you not to play with fire
But you couldn't resist the twisted desire
To play your games with me
My love leaves an imprint
A hole that you'll never be able to fill
You will always feel my absence
And i hope that emptiness makes you ill
You liked my porcelain skin
But not the anger that bubbled within
And now you will never escape
From the things you did to me

I Miss You But I Shouldn't

Do you ever wonder how I am?
Do you still think of us too?
Do you ever want to talk again?
Do you miss me like I do you?

Everyone tells me I'm better off
But I still find myself missing
The friendship we used to have
And I can't stop reminiscing

Maybe it was because you stuck around for so
long
Or because you saw me at my worst
And in terms of decent friends
You were a great one at first

I thought you'd be in my life longer
That we would grow old together
I thought I meant more to you
That you meant "best friends forever"

I'm sorry for the things I said
When I was angry at you
I still wish for you the best
No matter what we went though

My heart does ache when I think of
The way things could have been
I wish we could've fixed it
But I guess we can't always win

You threw away years of friendship
Based purely on lies
The way you never even cared
How I felt took me by surprise

I never asked you to pick sides
I tried not to bring you into it
But clearly you and her
Didn't share that same sentiment

So I don't know why it's so hard
For me to not see you as good
I don't know why I can't accept
How low priority I stood

Do you regret choosing her over me?
I think one day you will
Or you will spend the rest of your life
Supporting her while you stand still

I would have elevated you
Any way I knew how
I would've done anything for you

But that's not the case now

I am still angry at you
But in me there is a part
That wishes you would come back
To the place for you still in my heart

What I would give to hear you say
"I'm sorry and I miss you."
I might forgive you if you said
"I should have believed you."

But deep down I know the truth
That I can never let you back in
I will never be able to trust you again
Not after what you did

So I will sit with your memory
Knowing that's all I'll ever have
I'll love who you used to be
Because I know I'll never get that back

Small

I have always wanted to be dainty, delicate
So soft and small you couldn't dream to hurt me
I wanted to be out of the way and convenient
As if that would somehow make me more
worthy
All my life I was told that my presence was a
burden
That others didn't have it in them to bear
I wanted to appear as fragile as I felt
So others would know to handle me with care
But I was always too loud, too much, too
difficult
A lost puppy bumbling around at your heels
When I wanted to be a doll on display
A picture perfect reflection of your ideals
But I always seemed to be too square and sharp
My temper either too hot or too cold
Even when I tried to smooth my edges
I was never soft enough to hold
So when you let me in your bed at night
I tried not to take up much space
I was glad that I could keep you warm
But I still knew I was out of place
Because once the sun came up I knew
The bed we shared would be too small

I would shrink to the edges of your vision
No longer worthy of space at all
So I softened myself to become more palatable
And tried my best to be easier to swallow
Splitting myself into bite sized pieces
Or emptying myself until I felt hallow
But in the end all I was to you
Was crumbs scattered on the floor
Something so minute it invoked irritation
My existence by itself was a chore
So when you swept me up and tossed me out
Like I was just waste you needed to get rid of
I pulled myself together and fed till I was whole
And decided to stop shrinking myself for love

I Believe In Magic

I always loved fairytales
Consumed with stories of magic and mythology
When the cold reality of life seeped in
I coped with fantastical ideologies

Spending my childhood always lost in a book
Traversing the worlds that words could build
Traveling from one universe to another
When my own one didn't seem to fulfill

I dreamed of being called away to somewhere
far
On a long journey to discover my purpose
Something to confirm I had a place somewhere
To prove that I wasn't completely worthless

I built expansive worlds that were better than my
own
Filled with magic and love and adventure
A world where love is unconditional
And free of doubt and pressure

I always hoped that there was something more
Some knight in shining armor to save the day
But the fairytales and dreams never came true

No Prince Charming came to whisk me away

I was told to be practical, to think of my future
That I was getting too old to fantasize
I was told by aged angry people
That life wasn't something to romanticize

As if escaping into the comfort of the
inconceivable
Is a privilege only used by the weak
As if everyone must succumb to life's cruelty
And forfeit the thrill of mystique

Everyone is drawn to the unknown
Everyone wants to know what they don't
Everyone wants more than they have
Everyone wants to figure it out on their own

Now that I am older
I try to balance my dreams with reality
I try to hold on to the magic of life
And maintain an optimistic mentality

I got fairy wings etched on my back
To embrace the child inside me
I make my own fantastical stories
To make other young girls happy

There is magic inside us all

In the way we think and feel
There is already so much wonder
In the experiences that are real

We just have to be able to find it
And embrace it when we do
We must expect the unexpected
And be comfortable with the new

It's Okay

It is okay to be the way you are
And for your love to burn like a shooting star
It is okay that you feel how you feel
And it is okay for you to move on and heal
It is okay to ask for space
And to take life at your own pace
It is okay to be slow to trust
It is okay to not want to be touched
You are allowed to want your boundaries
respected
There's nothing wrong with wanting to be
protected
It is okay to be angry about the past
You're not a failure for coming in last
It is okay to sit down and rest
It's alright if you're not always your best
It is okay to make mistakes
And it is okay for you to take breaks
It is okay to prioritize yourself
It is okay to take care of your health
It is okay to protect your peace
It is okay to have your own beliefs
You don't need to worry about your weight
I promise you that you look great
It is okay to not be perfect

It doesn't mean that you are defect
It's okay to wallow in your sadness
You can forgive yourself for your rashness
You're not the way you are on accident
It's okay that you're so passionate
You are smart and kind and empathetic
You can make anything feel poetic
The people you love are lucky to have you
How unfortunate for the people you outgrew
You are doing the best you can
It is okay to not have a plan
Just remember that with time comes solutions
It is okay to not immediately have a conclusion
You will continue to grow and learn
Yes you will sometimes get burned
But what is life without the lesson
What is improvement without progression
You still have time to find the answers
You only have to meet your own standards
This life belongs to you and no one else
It's okay to prioritize yourself

The Child Inside

One day, in your favorite place, you come upon
a child
Something about her strikes you as oddly
familiar
She looks over her shoulder as if danger is
imminent
And you realize that you used to be just like her
You sit her down and ask her why she's here
And she says she is in need of protection
And would you please give her a warm bed
And a home full of love and affection
I come from a place that is cold and empty
And I would just like to know if there is warmth
In this big and scary mess of a world
That only seems to offer storm after storm
So you tell this child, just wait until you're older
This suffering will not last forever
Just hold on for a little while longer
And I promise that things will get better
You take her to your home and wrap her up in a
blanket
Give her some tea and something sweet to eat
You brush her hair and listen to her problems
And comfort her until she falls asleep
Because she's just a child and she deserves love

Just like you did at her age
You wouldn't blame her for her pain
You wouldn't make her deal with your rage
So why do you neglect your inner child so?
Why don't you treat her with the same kindness?
The children we used to be do not just go away
They live on deep inside us
And when that child does not feel safe
You will not either
And unless you are kind to yourself
You will never reach her
So remember this child when you're struggling
And remember that she is you
Think of her and what she deserves
In everything that you do

To Heal

Treating your wounds has never been easy
Especially when you know there will always be
scars
You must put time into yourself and confront
your past
Which can be hard when peace is already so
sparse
It's much easier to just give into the pain
To accept it as an absolute and unending truth
To let it dominate our lives and perceptions
And let it steal away our freedom and youth
Because to heal means to come face to face
With the part of you that holds all of your shame
And doing so leaves you terribly vulnerable
With nowhere left for you to hold the blame
But the shame is a necessary part of the process
But it's something you must work through
So that you can learn from your mistakes
And gain the tools to become a better you
We all have bruises still tender to the touch
What matters is how we respond when someone
bumps them
You must be gentle and cautious with yourself
Instead of making your pain everyone else's
problem

Because those who love us deserve our best versions
And perhaps more importantly, so do we
It will take effort, commitment, and devotion
No improvement can be made immediately
But with patience and time you get to know yourself
You learn what sets you off and why it does so
You can address the issue and find a solution
And only then will you at last truly grow
Sometimes you'll stumble, you'll feel like a failure
But you must remember that you're doing your best
You may sometimes feel that you have lost your way
But all your work isn't wasted by a few missteps
There will always be work to do
There will always be progress to be made
But that is no reason to give up
That is no reason to be afraid
You must always strive to meet your potential
And should never doubt your capabilities
Because being the best version of yourself
Is one of life's most important responsibilities

Can I Be Loved?

I'll always try my best to be supportive and kind
To those who choose to have me in their lives
But when my thoughts are not on my side
Will I still be loved?

I try my best to do everything right
I try to be polite, to be a delight
But if I'm not always a beacon of light
Can I still be loved?

I pride myself in my fierce loyalty
I can make anyone feel like royalty
But when I fall victim to my anxiety
Am I allowed to be loved?

I make an effort to learn from every mistake
And think about the choices I make
But if I cannot always be brave
Do I deserve to be loved?

And I know I shouldn't blame myself for how I
feel
And that the things I went through were very
real
But when my wounds finally heal

Will I still be able to love?

I will not be shamed for prioritizing my needs
I refuse to be blamed for protecting my peace
So when someone inevitably leaves
Can I still try to love?

Because I am so tired of giving everything
To people who don't even think of my
well-being
So when I decide to spread my wings
Am I allowed to love?

I want to be loved despite my flaws
I want to feel like I belong
So if I decide to let down my walls
Do I deserve to love?

Stay

What if I run out of words? What if
The happiness I hold onto never returns?
What if I'm always like this? What if
The sickness in my head wins?
Will you still be patient and kind? Will you
Still be there to tell me it's all in my mind?
Will you promise not to give up on me? Will you
Promise me that you won't leave?
I know that I can be difficult. I know
That your love is a miracle.
I know that you deserve the best. I know
That your love isn't a test. But
What if you find better? What if
My expectations are too much pressure?
What if I really am too much? What if
I can never do good enough?
Will you be honest if I am? Will you
Still try to understand?
Will you be gentle with my heart? Will you
Still miss me when we're apart?
I know that I might not be worth it. I know
That I will never be perfect. But
What if I promise to always try? What if
I promise that my love will never die?

What if my love is something you have to work
for?
What if one day I decide to ask for more?
Will you be angry or will you listen? Will you
Be my friend or my opposition?
Will you try to understand how I feel? Instead of
Projecting onto me your own ideal?
I know that may be a lot to ask. I know
That may feel like an attack. But
I just want to be treated with fragility. I just
Want someone to believe in my capability.
I just need to be handled with care. And I just
Need you to be aware. That
I never wanted to hurt you. I never
Wanted to burn you
I am just damaged and slow to trust
Sometimes my emotions are hard to con front
But I will always come to my senses
I will eventually let down my defenses
So please just be patient and stay by my side
I promise I have so much to provide